SEASONS *of the Soul*

By

JANET SYAS NITSICK

Tate Publishing, LLC.

"Seasons of the Soul" by Janet Syas Nitsick

Copyright © 2006 by Janet Syas Nitsick. All rights reserved.

Published in the United States of America
by Tate Publishing, LLC
127 East Trade Center Terrace
Mustang, OK 73064
(888) 361–9473

Book design copyright © 2006 by Tate Publishing, LLC.
All rights reserved.

No part of this publication may be reproduced, stored in a retrieval system or transmitted in any way by any means, electronic, mechanical, photocopy, recording or otherwise without the prior permission of the author except as provided by USA copyright law.

All scripture quotations, except where noted, are taken from the Holy Bible, King James Version, Cambridge, 1769.

Scripture quotations marked "NIV" are taken from the Holy Bible, New International Version ®, Copyright © 1973, 1978, 1984 by International Bible Society. Used by permission of Zondervan Publishing House. All rights reserved.

ISBN: 1-5988639-2-4

Dedication

And he shall be like a tree planted by the rivers of water,

that bringeth forth his fruit in his season;

his leaf also shall not wither; and whatsoever
he doeth shall prosper.

(PSALMS 1:3)

I dedicate Seasons of the Soul to my father, former state Sen. George Syas, now deceased, who was much admired for his knowledge of Nebraska's constitution. My mother who taught me the art of hard work, grace and style. And to my husband, brother, two older sons and my recently departed aunt who supported me and gave me encouragement during troubling times. I also dedicate this book to my close high-school friends and other supportive friends who cared about me. Additionally, Seasons of the Soul is dedicated to College of St. Mary professors who renewed my interest in writing.

Acknowledgements

Giving thanks always for all things unto God and the Father,

in the name of our Lord Jesus Christ; . . .

(EPHESIANS 5:20)

Thanks go to my brother, George David Syas, Jr., for reviewing and making suggestions to my stories. His time and insight was greatly appreciated and helped make my stories better.

Additionally, I want to thank my husband, Paul Nitsick, who read each story numerous times even when he was so tired he barely could keep his eyes open. Without his help, this book would not be the best work possible.

Introduction

I first met Janet Nitsick as a student in my classes at the College of Saint Mary, Omaha, Nebraska. As I grew to know her, it was clear that she was a woman of faith, with a sympathetic soul and a cheerful disposition. I also learned how great a desire she had to write. I am pleased that she is continuing to fulfill that desire.

In this devotional book, Janet reveals how her Christian faith has supported her and her husband Paul in coping with and caring for their two autistic sons. To convey the experience and the spirit of struggle and its opportunities for growth, she interweaves epigraph, aphorism, scripture, poetry, and true and fictional stories with family photos and vignettes of the two of them as parents guiding, loving, and living with the boys.

Janet divides her exposition along seasonal lines, accentuating the circle of time in the natural world and connecting every piece of her story to the passage of time, illustrating the work of time in growth and change. She highlights the human need for a life of faith, and demonstrates how such faith teaches one to live joyously and productively, and to know that help in all situations lies in that faith.

The book, therefore, becomes more than a story of

two parents with two autistic children, important as that part is. It becomes a lesson on learning to live a Christian life, in whatever life one finds oneself.

- Barbara W. Rippey, Ph. D.
SCHOLAR IN RESIDENCE
COLLEGE OF SAINT MARY
OMAHA, NEBRASKA

Table of Contents

CHAPTER ONE: *Summer*

Autistic Sons Bring Struggles, Joy 13
The Game of Life 16
Family Boston Trip 20
Author Jane Pratt 24
The Knock 28

CHAPTER TWO: *Fall*

Squirrel Chatter 33
Cat Prowl 37
Letter to God 40
The Crystallized Stone 43
The Puzzle 46

CHAPTER THREE: *Winter*

Grandma's Cookies....................................51

Sweaters of Love...................................54

Andrew's Bowling..................................58

Charlie..60

Thanksgiving Day.................................66

CHAPTER FOUR: *Spring*

This Day will Always be Special............71

The Merry-Go-Round.......................74

The Wilted Easter Lily......................76

Little Fluffy.......................................80

Rose's Flower Garden.......................82

CHAPTER ONE: *Summer*

HOT MUGGY . . .

SWEAT POURING DOWN YOUR BACK

AND FACE

POOLS AND WATER SPLASHING . . .

"Some time later, Jesus went up to Jerusalem for a feast of the Jews. Now there is in Jerusalem near the Sheep Gate a pool, which in Aramaic is called Bethesda and which is surrounded by five covered colonnades. Here a great number of disabled people used to lie—the blind, the lame, the paralyzed. One who was there had been an invalid for thirty-eight years. When Jesus saw him lying there and learned that he had been in this condition for a long time, he asked him, 'Do you want to get well?'

'Sir,' the invalid replied. 'I have no one to help me into the pool when the water is stirred. While I am trying to get in, someone else goes down ahead of me.'

Then Jesus said to him, 'Get up! Pick up your mat and walk.' At once the man was cured; he picked up his mat and walked."

(JOHN 5:1–9, NIV)

At a 100-year-old church celebration in 1986, parents Janet and Paul Nitsick are dressed in 19th century clothing. With them are their two autistic children, Brad, 5, and Andrew, 2.

Autistic Sons Bring Struggles, Joy [1]

"Help!" said the eyes of my husband, Paul, as he stared glassy-eyed at me. He was submerged in the deep end of the hotel's swimming pool. Quickly, I swam over to him and reached up to pull my oldest autistic son, Brad, off of him.

But immediately after pulling him off of my husband, Brad wrapped his body tightly around my upper torso. The weight of his body caused me to fall deeper under the water. I thought I was going to die.

Suddenly from the side of the pool, a woman swam over to me and pulled him off of me. Brad did not see her coming or he might have become frightened and tightened his hold on me. She had approached us from behind. She then swam over to the side of the pool and lifted him up on the edge.

In the meantime, I caught my breath and swam over to where Brad was at. Paul was still catching his breath. The incident ended happily with all of us getting out of the pool safely.

But just as other children grow older and change, so do autistic children. Earlier in his life, Brad loved the water. But now, at age 15, he had become afraid of it. This was how Paul got himself into trouble.

He thought he could stand in the more shallow portion of the deep end of the swimming pool. But that, of course, was a bad assumption because Brad shook with fear

13

and in his fear and strength was able to propel them further into the deep water. Brad's story was similar to other children with infantile autism.

He developed normally, walked at one and was even the easiest to toilet train out of my two older children. Brad even spoke at one and a half years. Some of his words were "pretty," "light," "Brad," and "go."

But as with many autistic children, suddenly his development of language stopped, which included the speaking of those words. At first, we thought his lack of language was because he had different caregivers or due to other relatives who also had experienced delays in speaking. But this was not the case. Brad also reacted erratically to certain sounds.

At times, it seemed as if he did not hear at all—but at other times he seemed to hear too well.

There was an incident many years ago that proves this point. My husband and I had just sat down to watch the movie, "Superman." We were in the living room when the theme song began. Then, I heard Brad scream, and I ran upstairs to his bedroom. I found him with tears streaming down his face. That tune hurt his ears.

Incidents such as these caused us to have a series of hearing tests. All of these tests resulted in normal ranges of hearing. At the time, and perhaps still today, hearing tests could not detect if a person heard too well.

So we made an appointment with a psychiatrist to see if he could find out what was wrong with Brad. The psychiatrist diagnosed Brad with Pervasive Development Disorder, which is part of the autistic spectrum. "Treat him like you would a dog," the psychiatrist said to us during one of our visits. People's words hurt, and we seem to remember those.

Another problem was finding the right school for a child with autism. I could go on and on about the many problems we experienced in having an autistic child, but that would require a book. But I will say that we constantly dealt with issues related to his disability.

My younger child also had autism. But Andrew was totally different than Brad because he could talk. He also took some regular classes at school.

I found that people sometimes believe that those with autism are incapable of doing certain things. That was the case with Andrew. He proved those people wrong, however, a few years ago when he called me at work and carried on a short conversation.

"I had a hot dog for lunch, and I put some mustard and ketchup on it," was one of the things Andrew said during our talk. This was music to my ears. I was so proud of him! This showed me that sometimes it is the little things in life that mean a lot.

Circle

Walking in circles, he turns round and round,

Not knowing where he is bound,

But, through God's grace, he finds his place,

And stands ready for His heavenly embrace.

The Game of Life

Bob Greenwell knew how to win on and off the field. He was a former quarterback for the pro-team, Minnesota Tigers, leading the team to many victories which included winning the 1995 Super Bowl. Greenwell was proud of that achievement.

"That was a terrific game," he recently told a friend. "The team was down two touchdowns when I pitched the ball to Tom Brown. He ran in for a touchdown. Then in the last two minutes of the game I threw a 'Hail Mary pass' and connected with Jim Drewman in the end zone."

Jim and Bob were close friends on and off the field. Jim died last year when he stepped in front of a car after the two were drinking. Bob was not there when it happened because he left early, so he could sober up before his wife Mary got home.

"The family is falling apart because of your drinking," Mary told him prior to Jim's death. Bob began to hide his addiction.

He stashed bottles of hard liquor in the car's glove compartment and underneath his seat. Bob and his wife bought their five-acre country home two years earlier. It was perfect for their two young sons, Ray and Bill, and their three dogs.

Bob got into his bright, red Cadillac, forgetting to fasten his seat belt, and pulled out of the four-car garage onto the long, winding driveway. Today, he decided to take the scenic route to work. Bob owned a financial investment business. He pulled off to the side of the road and grabbed a bottle of liquor, taking a couple of swigs of it before driving down the country road.

Bob pushed down on the gas pedal, and the vehicle sped up to 75 miles an hour. The day was hot and muggy, so he loosened his tie. The dark, gray clouds loomed overhead. Rain wasn't in the forecast, but within minutes large droplets hit the windshield.

He turned on the wipers. He could not find the defroster because his eyes were blurry. Bob saw the stop sign ahead, then he pressed his foot hard on the brake. But the high rate of speed made it difficult for him to stop. So he missed the stop sign and hit a telephone pole. The impact made Bob's head lunge forward.

Initially, he struck the air bag before it deflated. Then he hit the steering wheel. Blood oozed down his face and on his shirt and pants.

When Bob opened his eyes, he saw flashing red lights. The sirens aroused him from his unconsciousness. Paramedics lifted him onto the stretcher and put him in the ambulance.

"He is in bad shape. Take him to Angel Wings Hospital. It's the closest," Bob heard a paramedic say.

Bob's life flashed before him. He thought of his childhood. He always had attended church, but long ago he discounted the importance of God in his life. Now though, with his life hanging in the balance, it mattered. He wondered whether he was going to heaven or hell.

Bob realized his life was empty. He had tried to fill that void with alcohol. *But the game of life is only won when you fill your body with the love of Jesus.*

God is our refuge
and strength,
a very
present help in
trouble.

(PSALMS 46:1)

Paul Nitsick stands next to autistic sons—Brad, 23, and Andrew, 20, —in downtown historical Boston in 2004.

Family Boston Trip

Andrew, my 19-year-old autistic son, sat next to me as the family waited for the plane to take off from Omaha's Eppley Airfield. We were headed for Boston. I sat next to the window while Andrew sat near the aisle.

His leg jerked up and down as he intermittently fastened and unfastened his seat belt. I tried to calm down his anxiety by telling him we soon would take off. My words, though, were in vain because within minutes Andrew darted off the plane. That was the beginning of several mishaps that occurred during our Boston trip of 2004.

My husband Paul ran after Andrew. Paul was sitting across the aisle with Brad, our oldest autistic son. I moved over next to him I wanted to make sure Brad did not get up. We did not know if Brad understood what was going on since he could not talk.

Paul caught up with Andrew. The two reboarded the plane. But the pilot made them exit the cabin to undergo a new security check because Andrew ran onto the tarmac. Minutes seemed like hours as I waited for Paul and Andrew to again reboard.

"We understand your son did not do this deliberately," the stewardess said. "But we may have to boot the whole family off the plane." I panicked. Paul spent too many days planning this trip for it all to come to a quick end.

My brain surged into gear! "Andrew could sit next to

the window with Paul in the outside seat," I told her. "That way, my husband could make sure Andrew would stay seated."

Security officials agreed. Soon we took off—surprisingly only about 20 minutes late. We landed at Boston's Logan International Airport three hours later. Then we rented a car, and I drove it to Danvers, Mass.

From there, we visited Boston's Freedom Trail, toured Martha's Vineyard and went on a whale watch. Although we never saw any humpback whales, we did see its related counterpart—dolphins. That made Andrew happy.

I drove the family to Plymouth, where we saw Plymouth Rock and went inside the Mayflower replica. We then proceeded to Hyannis on Cape Cod. The next day we visited several Cape Cod villages, including Orleans the home of Rock Harbor.

I parked the car and grabbed my camera. We walked over to the harbor to get a better view. I decided to take some close-up pictures. I stepped into the water. Then placed my purse on an upper rock near the shore. I just finished taking a couple of pictures when high tide came in.

The waves rose to my knees and splashed onto the ledge where I put my purse. The tide drenched my purse, including our airline boarding passes, my checkbook and the Omaha Eppley Airport's parking stub. Paul dried out the boarding passes and the checkbook. But the flimsy, lightweight parking stub was ruined. That created a problem because without the stub, Omaha airport parking officials wanted us to pay almost triple the normal $24 weekly rate.

"But the stub was ruined when my purse got drenched during high tide," I told the parking attendant.

"I will talk with the manager," she replied. The attendant returned about 10 minutes later, telling us the manager agreed to have us pay the usual rate. We were grateful.

Prior to that, though, the family had another problem. Brad had a grand-mal seizure while on our return flight home. "Is there anything we can do to help?" the flight attendant asked.

"I will need a wheelchair when we land," I replied. An airport employee met us with the wheelchair. Paul took it from him. He put Brad in it, wheeling him down to the luggage area.

My husband then rented a luggage cart and placed our luggage on it. I took the wheelchair, and Paul pushed the cart. Andrew carried two suitcases. We walked toward the long-term parking lot.

The van, though, was difficult to locate because it was dark. And there was no parking stub to help us find it. We walked back and forth, locating it about 15 minutes later. Paul put Brad in the back seat and fastened his seat belt. Then he walked over to where Andrew and I stood ready to load the luggage. Paul grabbed the suitcases and put them into the trunk area. I just was relieved the whole trip was over.

Slowly, I walked toward the front, got into the driver's seat and adjusted my seat belt. I wanted to insert the key into the ignition, but didn't know if I had the energy to do it. I sighed. Then, I looked over at my husband and said: "Now, I really need a vacation." He laughed. Then I drove the family home.

Blessings

God's blessings come in

packages, large and small,

Untie the bow and break the string,

To see,

What He has in store,

For thee.

Author Jane Pratt

Author Jane Pratt took off her dress and neatly hung it on a hanger. She just returned from speaking at a local writers conference. Pratt told participants how she became an author.

"It takes hard work and persistence to get beyond the numerous rejection slips. But if you believe in your story, and it is well written. The book should sell," she told attendees.

Jane's life took many turns before she—at age 51—decided to pursue her heart's desire. The urge to be an author began as a child. Life, though, presented her with many obstacles, such as being a divorced single mother of two and later remarrying and having two autistic children.

With each trial, she gathered strength. That added strength gave her the ability to quit her full-time job and work part-time. In that way, she could put all her energy toward the dream, which was fulfilled three years ago. Pratt often opened a file-cabinet drawer full of rejection slips to remind her of her struggle. She was one of today's premier authors.

She wrote adult, teen and children's books. Each new release spelled success, which wore well on Pratt. She was humbled by it. God was the instrument that made it happen.

Today, Jane will meet her brother Bob at her Mom's home. The siblings were clearing out the house to get it ready for sale. Her mother had dementia.

So Bob and Jane placed her in a highly-recommended

nursing facility. Mom Polly loved the place. Activities kept her busy from morning to night. She was in great physical shape.

Jane hated rummaging through her Mom's belongings. It didn't seem right. "These are her things," she told Bob as she sorted through a box of papers. Her mother, however, was no longer capable of deciphering junk from important materials.

Jane looked out the large picture window. The view reminded her of summer days of softball, kick the can and other activities. A tear trickled down her face as she remembered her Dad, now deceased, and a beloved aunt who lived down the street. She died a month ago.

Jane stretched out on the couch and laid there for several minutes. She planned to take a short nap. But the stillness jogged her memory. "I wonder if it still is here?" she yelled to her brother. He was in Mother's bedroom. Jane ran toward the basement steps.

"I do not know what you are talking about." Bob replied.

"Come down with me to the basement, and you will see." Jane went straight for Mom's old hope chest, lifted the lid and searched through blankets and old sewing materials. "It's here! I feel the metal box," she said as she pulled out an old lunch box plastered with gold-star stickers. She opened the latch.

The letters still were inside. "I wrote letters to God," Jane said. "The letters asked Him to make me an author when I grow up." *God also will answer your prayers if only you trust in Him.*

Behold,

I stand at the door,

and knock:

if

any man hear my voice,

and open the door,

I will come in

to him, and will sup with him,

and he with me.

(REVELATION 3:20)

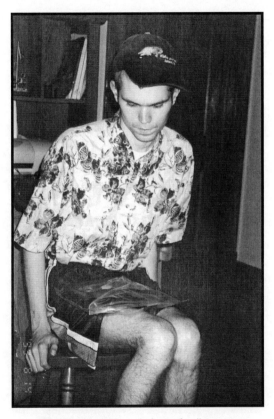

Brad Nitsick sits in a chair at a family event.

The Knock

Paul and I were watching a television program when we heard a knock on our door. It was our neighbor. "Brad is out. My daughter-in-law saw him walking down the street," he said.

Brad, 23, was our oldest autistic son. He did not talk nor did he fear danger. I raced out the door and started to run down Main Street in Springfield, Nebraska. Paul could not immediately join the search. He had to hunt for his shoes.

Brad had escaped from our home before. But this time it was worse because, according to the neighbor, he was out for many minutes. (The neighbor's daughter-in-law did not know our name or telephone number. But she did know where we lived, which was next to her in-laws. So it took time for her to contact her in-laws and for them to get in touch with us.)

The delay gave Brad time to walk across the small town and even get to Nebraska Highway 50. I jogged about a block when a woman yelled, "I know where he is. Get in my van, and I will take you to him." She had just dropped off her daughter at the local Catholic church near us for catechism lessons.

I knew the elementary school teacher. I talked with her when I was a reporter for a local newspaper. She also was familiar with my family since she saw us at several town functions. She drove me to R and R Bar, which is about a half mile away. Brad stood outside the door. The blaring music probably drew him to the place.

The teacher lived close to the bar. The woman drove her van into the parking lot. I got out.

"Brad," I yelled as I walked toward him. I grabbed his hand and pulled him to the van. She drove us home. Thanks to caring neighbors Brad was safe, and for that we forever are grateful.

But later, Paul and I wondered how he got out of the house. We checked all the locks before we sat down to watch TV. We got our answer several days later. It came when Paul observed Brad turning the screen door lock. It was something he never did before.

Sometimes, we believe special children stop learning. But these children learn just like the rest of us. *They are God's creation.*

CHAPTER 2: *Fall*

SCHOOL...
LEAVES BLOWING
A CHILL IN THE AIR...

Where Did the Time Go

Once it was summer—

The lazy days of talking to neighbors

and watching our gardens grow,

Where did the time go?

Once it was fall—

With leaves turning to bright reds and yellows

and children returning to school,

Where did the time go?

Once it was winter—

Snow and ice covered the ground with trees barren

and fireplaces aglow,

Where did the time go?

Once it was spring with flowers budding and

birds reappearing—

Where did the time go?

It rolled right back to its past just as God planned it to go.

Squirrel Chatter

Brownie ran across the large yard. He loved to play. He especially loved playing with Chunky, his best friend. Brownie and Chunky played throughout the summer. Sometimes the squirrels challenged each other to a race. "Let's see who can make it first to the big walnut tree at the end of the yard," Brownie told Chunky.

But to Brownie and Chunky, it did not matter who won the race. It was fun being together. The squirrels enjoyed playing "tail high."

"Tail high" was a game they invented. The object was to lift their tails as high as they could while they ran across the grass. Sometimes they even played the game at night and watched their tails' shadows in the moonlight.

But now, the days were getting shorter. They had to go to bed earlier. Soon, they would start "squirrelly" school. Classes were held in a large, deep hole inside a walnut tree. Chunky knew he would miss playing games with his friend. But school was important. At school, the two would learn how to gather and store nuts for winter.

"Look for a tree that is full of nuts," the teacher said. "Then run on its branches and swish your tail so that the nuts fall to the ground. It is crucial to gather plenty of nuts for winter."

Brownie listened to her words. But he wanted to run and play, so Brownie gathered only a few nuts. Chunky, on the other hand, obeyed his teacher.

September turned to October. It now was difficult for Brownie to play because the sun went down shortly after school. But instead of Brownie gathering more nuts, he dreamed of summer and playing with Chunky.

"Winter soon will be here. You need to gather nuts," Chunky said. Brownie, however, did not listen.

Now it was December. Brownie and Chunky no longer went to school. They learned all they needed to know. The first snowfall came on Christmas Day. It was a light, fluffy snow and although there was an inch on the ground, Brownie still found a few nuts.

Then, January rolled in and the ground was covered with ice and snow. Brownie no longer could go outside. He had to survive on the small amount of nuts he had gathered. Chunky, though, had plenty of nuts.

Finally, spring came. The birds returned to sing their melodies. Chunky began to play outside.

"Where is my friend?" he thought. Then he saw Brownie. He was lying next to a tree.

Brownie lost weight. His head drooped. Chunky ran to him. He carried a glass of water with a large nut curled inside his tail.

"I learned my lesson," Brownie said after drinking the water and eating the nut. "From now on, I will listen to my teacher and friends. I will do what I am told."

Is God your teacher? Are your listening and doing what He would want you to do?

34

The Door

Oh! Wooden door why do you stand there,

Trying to not let the light come in?

Keeping me from the Man who saved mankind,

And who washed away my sins.

The family cat

Cat Prowl

Temperatures were in the upper 60's. And red, yellow and brown leaves covered the ground the day our family searched the house for Andrew's cat. Andrew always put the cat in his room before he went to bed.

The cat had long hair, a mixture of cocoa-brown and white, and green eyes. The family had gotten quite accustomed to his friendly personality. He loved to jump on your lap or snuggle next to you while you lay in bed. The cat became part of our family a few years ago, after Andrew woke up one morning and found his former cat, Golden, had died.

Andrew was devastated, especially since we just moved into our new house. The cat was his only friend. Thankfully, my former boss was looking for a home for his daughter's cat. His son-in-law and daughter were moving into his house. The newlyweds wanted to save money. But my boss did not want the cat.

So, we took the cat. At first, the cat was not happy with his new living arrangements. He ran underneath Andrew's bed and hissed at us when we approached. My husband Paul was the one who calmed the beast.

It happened this way. The cat wandered into the upstairs bathroom. My husband was in there. He quietly approached the cat and started to pet him. The rest was history.

So, when Andrew said, "I can't find my cat," we were worried. Paul looked under beds, in the basement and behind window curtains. Later, I joined the search. I examined opened dresser drawers and closets.

"I know he was in our bedroom about an hour ago," I told my husband. Even though we could not see how he could have gotten outside, we feared the worse because he was declawed. "Could he defend himself?" we wondered. After a lengthy search, we gave up and went to bed.

It was around 6 a.m. when my husband heard a bang at Brad's bedroom door. (Brad is autistic and cannot talk. If we did not lock his door at night, he could wander off or have a grand-mal seizure while walking down the stairs.) Brad knocked on his door when he wanted out. Because of that, my husband expected to find Brad when he opened the door.

But instead there was Faith, the cat. He probably hid in a back corner underneath Brad's bed. *Faith is it missing in your life? Remember God stands ready to open the door for you.*

Make a joyful noise unto the Lord,

all the earth:

make a loud noise, and rejoice,

and sing praise.

(PSALMS 98:4)

Aunt Dorothy Geiger examines a gift at a family Christmas party in 2003.

Letter to God

Sept. 7, 2005

To: God
Address: Heaven
Dear God:
Subject: An Unsung Hero

Aunt Dorothy sang out of tune. That, however, did not stop her from singing in church or joining in sing-alongs. She loved music. I remember kidding her about her inability to sing. She took it good-naturedly; just like she did everything.

Dorothy died Aug. 2, 2005—the day of our 25th wedding anniversary. She and my mother, Pauline, were close. Pauline, 92, was the last of the Paul and Grace Crowder family, which included Mom, Dorothy, Eleanor and Tommy. Dorothy was Pauline's stabilizing force in her later years.

Mom had dementia. So when Mom could not find her keys or purse, Mom called Dorothy. Then Dorothy walked the block to her house. Usually, Dorothy found nothing because Mom placed lost items in unbelievable places, such as a purse later discovered underneath the kitchen sink.

Dorothy also reminded Mom of family gatherings. Mom was unable to remember the times or dates. The two complimented each other in other ways, too, because Mom had good eyesight and Dorothy's was failing.

Of course, the siblings fought too. Mom resented Dorothy's constant reminders. However, through it all, the two stayed close.

Mom even wanted Dorothy to join her at Brighton Gardens, a nursing facility in Omaha. Mom went to live there in July of 2005. Dorothy, though, did not make it. For many years, Dorothy rebounded from asthma attacks and heart problems. In the end, however, she could not overcome a series of strokes.

Dorothy was my surrogate mother and my confidante and friend. She knew how to persevere—overcoming the death of three husbands. Her first husband, Darrell or nicknamed Dip (I do not know why), was her most beloved.

Dorothy, though, was our beloved. She cared. She loved and showered us with joy. No, Dorothy could not sing in tune. But she was our unsung hero.

Thank you Lord for her service,
Janet Syas Nitsick, her niece

The Dark

Glowing in the Dark,

they gathered with evil,

To destroy and pound the nails.

Screams of glee, the crowd did cry,

Then darkness and gloom came over the sky.

But a shining light,

Broke through the night,

Spelling out His saving grace,

Opening His hands for all to embrace.

The Crystallized Stone

The Middle Ages was a time of knights and chivalry. Most people also believed in witches and goblins. Let us go back to that time.

Two figures dressed in black poured water into a cauldron. "We need to search the forest to find ingredients for our brew," Delilah said. With that, Delilah and Jackoline grabbed their knives and headed for the Dark Forest. Most travelers avoided going there. For it was said the devil lived there.

The two picked their way through tree branches, vines and weeds. Not much else grew in the gloomy land. Soon, Jackoline spied a snake. It crawled out from underneath a jagged rock.

"I bet there are more underneath," Jackoline yelled as she pushed it over. "Wonderful! Wonderful!" she squealed as she found a nest of poisonous snakes. With her knife, she stabbed each viper and placed them inside her bag. "Serpents give the brew a nice, tangy flavor, " she said.

The women continued their search. Then they came across a row of mushrooms. "Oh! How delicious," Delilah said as she pulled up the poisonous toadstools, placing them into her bag. The two proceeded until they reached a large rock. "Let's sit here," Delilah said. And that was where they rested their wretched bodies.

Years ago the women had smiley faces and hearts of gold. But that changed when jealousy overcame them. They were envious of Crystal.

Crystal had a voice as sweet as droplets of rain upon a rose bush. And her golden curls sparkled in the sun. Crystal was the person villagers called when a child was sick or someone needed comforting. This angered Delilah and Jackoline. So they made a pact with the devil to destroy her, and destroy her they did.

"A child is sick inside the forest. She needs your help," they told her. Crystal believed them. She walked into the forest. An evil lumberjack awaited her. He slashed her with his ax. Vultures ate her remains.

The devil's pact required Delilah and Jackoline to make Satan a brew every day. Failure to do so would mean their death. The witches continued their journey.

They looked for a special rock. The two found a sparkling, crystallized stone near a dead log and returned to the cauldron. Delilah and Jackoline threw each ingredient into the pot, waiting until the end to add the stone.

Goodness, though, overcame evil because the crystallized stone represented Crystal's soul. And that beautiful soul consumed the ugly, evil ingredients. *Evil also could consume us if we do not follow Jesus.*

Puzzle Pieces

Scattered,

the puzzle pieces lay,

Ready to arrange and mold as clay.

But the pieces do not mesh,

Until God guides the faltering flesh.

The Puzzle

Christa sorted through the puzzle pieces. She searched for the last border piece before she connected the other pieces. Putting puzzles together was therapy for the intelligent, sweet woman.

This time, though, her mind wandered. She had too much trauma in her life recently. It started with the death of her beloved aunt, who died two months ago. Next, it was her mother who no longer could live in her house. Her dementia made that impossible.

So Christa took her in for awhile. But that became difficult because Mom needed constant activities. And Christa just could not provide that. After a month-long search, however, the siblings found her a beautiful assisted-living facility. It provided her with many activities. Now, Christa faced another problem—it was her job. She was a journalist.

Christa loved meeting and interviewing people then writing the articles. She was a good writer and knew how to find stories. However, this did not help her with her abusive editor.

The situation started to deteriorate two years earlier, when Bea, another reporter, and Christa no longer got along. Offices often have situations like this. But Bea controlled John, the editor, and he was determined to get rid of her. Nothing was going to interfere with his favorite reporter. Bea wanted her gone.

Christa sought help from other professionals within the company. The situation, however, continued to escalate with the editor's constant yelling, snide remarks and jubilation if he thought he got her on something. Christa finally quit at age 58.

"Now, what am I going to do?" she cried. "Newspaper journalism jobs are difficult to find. Especially today," she sighed, "with dips in circulation and less paid advertisements."

She knew her stories appealed to readers. This was because readers and sources often told Christa how much they loved her work. "You are an excellent reporter," one source told her. "You get the story right—which didn't happen in the past—and you are a good writer."

Christa took comfort in those words. She just did not know how to proceed. "If only I was 15 years younger," Christa thought.

She was putting together a 12-inch by 36-inch panoramic picture puzzle of Colorado. The puzzle-box lid showed a restful scene of streams and mountains. "Boy! Do I wish I could be there," she thought.

Christa *continued* to look for that particular border piece. Finally, she found it near a light blue angular one. "And the Lord shall *guide* thee *continually,* and satisfy thy soul in drought, and make fat thy bones: and thou shalt be like a watered garden, and like a spring of water, whose waters fail not." (Isaiah 58:11)

CHAPTER THREE: *Winter*

COLD WINDS . .

SNOW

FIREPLACES AGLOW . . .

*And in the sixth month the angel Gabriel was sent from God
unto a city of Galilee, named Nazareth,*

To a virgin espoused to a man whose name was Joseph,
of the house of David;

and the virgin's name was Mary.

And the angel came in unto her, and said, Hail,
thou that art highly favoured,

the Lord is with thee: blessed art thou among women.

And when she saw him, she was troubled at his saying, and
cast in her mind what manner of salutation this should be.

And the angel said unto her, Fear not,

Mary: for thou hast found favour with God.

And behold, thou shalt conceive in thy womb,

and bring forth a son,

and shalt call his name JESUS.

He shall be great, and shall be called the Son of the Highest;

and the Lord God shall give unto him the
throne of his father David.

And he shall reign over the house of Jacob for ever;

and of his kingdom there shall be no end.

(LUKE 1:26–33)

Grandma's Cookies

Joey Lynn remembered his grandmother telling him to wipe the chocolate off his face. Joey loved his Grandma Blessing's chocolate-chip cookies. Each Christmas his grandma made him two dozen of the tantalizing treats. That gift was his favorite because it came from his grandmother's heart. She was poor and unable to buy him a present.

Grandma would not be joining Joey's family for Christmas this year. She died of a heart attack eight days before Christmas. Joey thought about his grandmother as Christmas Day approached, remembering the cookies placed in a tin can and wrapped in aluminum foil.

Grandma always put the cookies toward the back of the tree, so it would be the last present unwrapped. She wrote his name on the gift tag. But she gave Joey the present personally.

Just a day before her death, Grandma ate dinner with Joey's family. The family laughed as Grandma told them about the time Dad and Uncle Cliff tried to run away. Dad and Cliff were mad because Grandma made them clean the house. But Grandpa Don, now deceased, found them about two blocks away. Punishment was two weeks of no television.

Grandma's smile and good-natured personality made everyone love her. She often kidded Joey about his wiry, red hair and freckles. "Those freckles look like strawberries," she said, "and I love strawberries."

When Joey was younger, Grandma would gently kiss him on the cheek. But now that he was nine-years-old she had avoided what Joey called, "the mushy stuff." Joey wrapped his last present. It was his grandmother's gift. He decided to give the pot holders to his mother.

Joey's family almost decided not to have Christmas at their house this year. But Dad's relatives liked their big house. Everyone also loved his Mom's homemade fudge.

Uncle Cliff and Aunt Betsy and their daughters—Sherrie and Gracie—were the first to arrive. He wished his cousins were boys because the girls wanted him to play house. Soon, the rest of the family arrived. Dinner included smoked turkey, corn, baked beans and homemade bread.

Sherrie and Gracie distributed the presents. Gracie gave Joey a big box. It was the race track he wanted.

The big grandfather's clock ticked off the hours. Relatives laughed and talked about their jobs, the past and upcoming events and, of course, Grandma. Scattered across the floor were wrapping paper, bows and ribbons. Joey noticed one present still under the tree.

He reached for it. It had his name on it. He unwrapped it. Inside was a tin can of chocolate-chip cookies. Joey knew who gave him that gift. It was his grandmother. She placed the present under the tree when she visited them. *Even in death, Grandma Blessing reached out and reminded Joey of her love. The same is true of God. He always is there with His blessings and His love for you.*

The Mountain

I stand at the foot of the mountain

And do not see,

What God has in store for me.

But after I climb to the mountain's top cliff,

A breeze gives me a fresh lift,

It cools my body

and my soul—

And soothes my mind,

to the land below

Where I leave my troubles behind.

And raise my face,

To be held and wrapped in God's heavenly embrace.

Sweaters of Love

Mary sat in her rocking chair and clicked the needles together as she knitted an infant sweater. Although her hands were worn and rough, her touch with the needle never left her. Mary made many sweaters and blankets over the years, but this one especially meant a lot. Her youngest son, Frank, and his wife, Carrie, just had their first child—a daughter.

"Children are such blessings," she thought. With the birth of this child, Mary had two granddaughters and one grandson. The other grandchildren were by her oldest son, Brian. Mary knitted each of Brian's children a sweater.

Grandmother's sweaters were a family tradition. No sweater, however, was the same because each bore a different design unique for each child. Mary knitted a lavender sweater with a small violet flower on its front for her first grandchild, Jolleen. The violet appliqué was designed by her, patterned after the violets that grew in her flower bed.

Mary was ten years younger then and her hands and face were not as wrinkled. She smiled as she thought of Jolleen when she was four. Mary took her outside to help water the flowers. That day was blustery at first, then the winds suddenly stopped.

Mary told Jolleen about how the weather changed. "Grandma," Jolleen said. "God is a big guy. He will do whatever He wants."

Grandma put the sweater down to eat lunch. "Let's

see," she thought. "I believe I have some leftover chicken on the top shelf of the refrigerator." Mary felt for the chicken, which was behind a jar of jelly. She grabbed a piece of chicken. Then she took it to the kitchen table.

After lunch, Mary picked up her needles and knitted for an hour before taking a short nap. The sun was not as bright when she started to again wrap the yarn around the needle. Mary was glad Frank and Carrie named their daughter Elizabeth. It fit because the name meant God's promise and showed the importance of faith in her son and daughter-in-law's lives. She also was thankful her eldest son was raising his children in the Lord.

Mary knitted a white sweater laced with threads of gold. The gold reminded her of the city of gold that awaited believers in Heaven. She clicked the needles together, knitting several rows until she came to the last stitch. She grabbed the other sweater pieces, lying next to her chair. Then she sewed the pieces together.

"It is beautiful," she thought. Mary lifted the receiver of the old-fashioned rotary phone and dialed Frank. He answered. "I finished it," she told him.

Mary, though, could not see the present she made. She had been blind for three years. It was God who guided her fingers. But it was her "seeing" heart that knitted the sweater. *God also has knitted a garment of love for you when you open your eyes to Him.*

They that sow in

tears

shall reap in joy.

(PSALMS 126:5)

Autistic son, Andrew Nitsick, and mother, Janet, stand inside Wildcat Lanes in Papillion, Neb., after Andrew won a gold medal in the state's Special Olympics Bowling Tournament in 2005.

Andrew throws his lightweight bowling ball down the alley.

Andrew's Bowling

My son's bowling score probably was nothing to shout about. Most people even would consider it a disgrace. To my 20-year-old autistic son, however, it was something special. His score won him a gold medal during the state Special Olympics Bowling Tournament in 2005. Several Omaha and area bowling alleys hosted the event.

Andrew bowled at Wildcat Lanes in Papillion, the place where he bowled with other Papillion-LaVista Special Olympians throughout the year. His yearly average was 75. He qualified for the state games in January. We were so proud of him.

Andrew bowled in that special league for several years. But in 2005 he found a secret weapon—a lightweight bowling ball. Most balls were too heavy for his thin, lanky build. So he could not aim the ball with accuracy. Marge Volpert, Papillion-LaVista Special Olympics coach, found the ball for him and away Andrew went—making strikes and spares like never before. After Andrew received his medal, he smiled, which is sometimes difficult for autistics to do.

Great athletes, though, often thank others for their success. We want to thank his coach. And Robbie Hurst, bowling manager of Wildcat Lanes, who gave Andrew the ball. God bless them, and God bless Andrew.

Charlie

Charlie! Charlie!

Is the name,

The fireman said as he brushed the horse's mane.

Animal and man inseparable,

That is unmistakable.

Charlie

Little petals of snow fell upon the brick pavement. It was Omaha's second snowfall in the year 1919. Downtown businesses lights shined in the dark night.

Owen Sias, nicknamed Red for his red hair, stood next to his favorite horse, Charlie. Red cared for the firehouse's team of horses but had a special attachment to Charlie. The two had been together since he became an Omaha fireman seven years before.

Every day during the winter Red fed Charlie an apple— saved from his apple tree. Red wiped the apple upon his pants and put it to Charlie's mouth. The horse hurriedly ate it.

"Red, are you in the barn?" asked fireman Orville.

"Yes," Red replied.

"You and that horse. It is a wonder your wife is not jealous of him." Orville said.

Red loved his wife, Edith. The couple married in 1904. The two fell in love at first sight and six months later they were married. The couple had three children.

Each child was a little different. George, the oldest, was self-assured and attended high school. If he finished school, it would be quite an achievement because not many children completed twelve years of school. Fathers needed the children to work the fields or to go to work to bring in extra income. Kenneth, aged nine, was their second child, and Irene was their youngest at age seven.

Red thought about his children as he brushed Charlie's coat. Kenneth was mischievous. He reminded Red of himself in his younger days. "Don't hide Irene's dolls," Red scolded Kenneth last night. But what he could not tell his son was how he too had tormented his younger sister. Red pulled his sister's pigtails and grabbed her long skirt—when he was a child.

Red was a violinist in an Omaha orchestra. But, Edith did not like Red to play the violin. She said it disturbed the children. So Red obeyed her wishes and played it for Charlie. The instrument soothed Red's nerves, and Charlie swished his tail at the first note. Red stored the violin in the hay loft.

Winter indeed had settled upon the Midwest. But the coldest was yet to come. When it did come, Red ceased playing. His fingers could not stay warm long enough to move the bow. Suddenly, an alarm bell rang.

Red hitched the horses while the rest of the fire crew climbed into the wagon. The Harney Hotel, 11th and Harney, was in full blaze when the firemen arrived. Red saw one man's head leaning outside a third-floor window.

"There is a man up there. Get the ladder, and I will go up!" Red said. No sooner had Red climbed the ladder and helped the man down when the men heard the second floor start to collapse.

"Four men are dead!" yelled one fireman after several firefighters pulled the bodies outside. Stations No. 1, 2 and 15 also responded, but all arrived too late. Thankfully, most patrons got out in time. The firemen sprayed water on the building's debris, making sure all flames were extinguished.

"What a night," thought Red. But silently he was

proud the company arrived on the scene in minutes. "Charlie always is ready to go. He responds with calm, swift speed. I do not see that in the other horses," Red told fellow fireman, Marvin.

Red unhitched the horses. Then led them into their stalls. "I will give them some hay for the night," Red told the men.

"Just do not spend the night with them," quipped James. The men loved kidding Red about his relationship with the horses.

A tear fell down Red's cheek. He quickly wiped it off with his handkerchief. "It is unmanly to cry," Red uttered underneath his breath.

The coal-stove fire started to go out. So Red added a few more chunks of coal. Red was tired and weary. He stretched out his body on the hard cot. No more alarms occurred that night.

A rooster's crow woke up the men. Red hated to get up, not because of his tiredness. Instead, he dreaded what the day had in store for him and the crew.

Yesterday's snow, melted in two pails by the stove, provided a fresh water supply for the horses. Red carried the water with trembling hands into the barn. The horses drank from the pails. Usually, Red played the violin at night. But today was different.

He felt for the wooden case and pulled it down from the loft. Charlie munched upon last night's hay. Red plucked the strings to prepare his fingers for play. The day was a little warmer so his fingers worked fast.

"What should I play?" Charlie gave him a gentle nudge. "Yes, that would be a good tune," Red said. "Blest be the tie that binds our hearts in Christian love. The fellowship of kindred minds is like to that above."

Outside he heard the motorized vehicle pull up to the firehouse. The men started to exit the station. Red knew within minutes he too would leave.

Red played and sang the last verse. "When we asunder part, it gives us inward pain. But we shall still be joined in heart and hope to meet again."

With shaking hands, Red ran his fingers over Charlie's coat. "Good-bye," he said softly. Then he left the barn.

Red stood outside as the motorized fire truck pulled up to the station. Oil spilled upon the pavement. The horses were being replaced with the new motorized vehicle. The men were apprehensive about it, hearing bad tales from other firemen.

The city's fire commissioner sensed the firemen's mood. "You will get used to the new equipment. The money saved from the care of the horses will allow the department to raise your salaries," he said. The commissioner looked over at Red. He heard how much Red loved the horses. Commissioner Tom Brown had a surprise.

"Red! The department is giving you Charlie. Take him home with you tonight."

Red simply smiled. He had to stay composed.

That night Red led Charlie out of the stall. Red wished he could ride him home, but he needed to purchase a saddle first. So the two walked home.

It started to snow. Flakes fell on their backs and necks as Red hummed: "When we asunder part, it gives us inward pain. But we shall still be joined in heart, And hope to meet again." [2–8]

Thanksgiving

Thanksgiving is a blessed time of sharing,

And gathering of kin,

A time to start the Christmas

shopping,

And wear a seasonal pin.

It is a time of hope,

And to look forward to a new year,

Don't take time to mope,

Just wallow in good cheer.

Janet Nitsick hugs her granddaughter Colleen with granddaughter Bridget in the background at a family event in 2004. Janet has three granddaughters and one grandson.

Thanksgiving Day

I just had put the turkey in the oven. Another Thanksgiving Day was fast upon us. Thanksgiving, of course, launched the Christmas season.

Soon I would buy gifts, make cookies and wrap presents. I looked forward to it. You doubt if you will get everything done, but usually you do. I put the Christmas compact disc in the CD player. The music would get the family in the holiday spirit. I was in good humor even with all I needed to do before relatives arrived. My thoughts went back to a Thanksgiving several years ago.

During that time, I was in college, pursuing a language-arts teaching degree. I was in the midst of writing several term papers when my husband, Paul, brought in the Thanksgiving turkey. "Where should I put it?" he asked.

"Put it on the counter," I replied.

He did.

I never thought anything more about it until three days later when I saw the turkey sitting on the counter. "Oh no! That turkey could have botulism. It could make everyone sick or even could kill them," I thought. Paul would not be happy if he had to buy another one. He had searched several grocery stores before finding this 18-pound turkey at an economical price.

I told my mother what happened. "I will buy you another one," she said. Mom walked in with the new turkey.

"What are you going to do with the old one?" I asked.

"I will put it in the Leavenworth Street dumpster." Mom said. (The dumpster was a few blocks from my Omaha home.) I was relieved. Mom called later.

"There was no room inside the dumpster," she said. "So I placed the turkey on the lid." People traveling down that street probably were shocked when they saw my turkey.

Years later, I told Paul about the incident. He laughed. It's difficult to admit you are as dumb as a turkey.

God, though, accepts you as you are. "Just as I am, thou wilt receive. Wilt welcome, pardon, cleanse, relieve because thy promise I believe. O Lamb of God I come! I come!" [9]

CHAPTER FOUR: *Spring*

GRADUATION . . .
FLOWERS GROWING
RAIN FALLING . . .

Graduation

A step slowly walks

across the stage–

To grasp a paper there,

To hear–

Applause and smiles

and cheers,

From all those held dear!

Touching the ground,

He moves around,

And sees a world of woe–

But worry not,

for God never will depart–

He is there always with His heart!

Brad, 21, wears a Benson High School graduation cap and gown in 2003.
Special education staff members took the photograph.

This Day will Always be Special

With tears in their eyes, fathers and mothers gathered for the graduation ceremony. It would be a day like no other. No more would my husband and I walk down the halls to my son's classroom. No more would we have conversations with teachers.

It was a new day not only for us, but for Brad. He would walk out of that classroom and face a brand new world. No, he would not be going to college—because he cannot talk nor can he write.

No, he would not be moving out on his own—because he always will need someone to take care of him. He would not drive a car or ride a bike or even hop on a skateboard. He could not do any of those things.

But the one thing he could do was kiss us and let us know in that small way that he loved us. And that was why it was so special to be part of his graduation pizza party. It was a small gathering of parents who joined us on May 22, 2003, as we all sat around eating pizza with the other special-education students.

The teacher had prepared a special large book titled, "This Book is About Me." The book contained photos of Brad in a green graduation cap and gown. Although we never would see him walk across the stage, it was still touching. It also had a digitalized photo of his face. To look at it, you would never know he was "special." Inside also was a large hand print, a forever remembrance of that day.

The substitute teacher tried to liven things up with a game of Truth or Consequences. "If you answer the questions correctly, you will not have to come back next year," said Teacher Donald Mardock. Out of 15 students, there were three graduates—Brad, Adam and Nick.

"What is the most beautiful melody?" Mardock asked.

"Row, Row, Row Your Boat," responded Adam. Nick beamed as he also got his question right. Then it was Brad's turn.

"Where is the garden spot where you live?" the teacher asked. Brad pressed the device's button. "Springfield," was the mechanical voice's response.

"Seniors do not have to come back next year," Mardock said.

No, the seniors will not be back because they will venture onto other paths, as other students do. Brad's will be a day program, where he will do simple tasks, such as put a nut onto a bolt. But in our hearts the "simple" low-key ceremony always will be special just as Brad will always be special to us.[10]

Merry-Go-Round

It spins and whirls round and round,

And, goes up and down.

Glistening in the sun,

The horses stand ready to run,

But instead, steady they stay,

So, little children can play.

Until it stops one day,

And, no longer those children play,

To prance,

and dance,

in the sun.

The Merry-Go-Round

Four-year-old Ruth grabbed her mother's hand as she walked toward the carnival rides. The fair was crowded. Ruth was scared. "Come on Ruth," her mother said. "Don't be afraid. Remember I have your hand."

Her mother's words gave her comfort. It was a beautiful spring day. The sun was bright and temperatures were in the upper 70's. The smell of popcorn was in the air.

May purchased tickets, then led her daughter to the children's rides. The daughter handed the attendant two tickets. She climbed into a little red boat which sat in a large, circular tank of knee-deep water. The boats circled several times around the tank before the attendant stopped the ride, and the children got off.

Ruth walked along with her mother. Several balloons floated in the air. "May I have a balloon, a beautiful yellow one?" Ruth asked.

Her mother smiled. She loved her little daughter. The mother bought Ruth a balloon, which was as bright as the sun.

"I will tie it around your wrist, so you don't lose it," May said.

"Oh Mother! Thank you. The balloon is beautiful."

Soon, they came to a row of food stands. "Let's get something to eat. It's past lunch time, and my feet ache," May said.

They sat down at a booth. Her mother bought them hamburgers, sodas and a large order of fries. Ruth sipped on the soda. Then she pulled the hamburger out of the bun and bit into it. Her mother thought about scolding her. But instead she remembered when she was a child and did not eat the bun.

May and Ruth walked down the fairway and watched people playing games. One father won a big, stuffed bear for his daughter. "Family, that is what makes life worth living," May thought. The merry-go-round was in front of them.

"Oh, Mother! Please may I ride the merry-go-round?" The mother looked for horses, where the two could ride side by side. She helped Ruth onto a beautiful horse decorated in shades of purple. Its head was etched in gold. The mother grabbed the reins of a red horse. It also was etched in gold. The attendant started the ride. And around the horses went as they moved up and down to the music.

Then, the ride stopped. Ruth climbed down from her horse. But she no longer was a little girl.

She now was a grown woman. Because, you see, the merry-go-round of life kept whirling round and round as daughters became mothers over and over again. Remember Mother's Day is in May. Tell your mother you love her.

For God so loved the world,

that he gave his only begotten Son,

that whosoever believeth in him should not perish,

but have everlasting life.

(JOHN 3:16)

The Wilted Easter Lily

Rev. Paul Thompson told parishioners to pick up an Easter lily after the service. Judy Gardner wanted to get one to decorate her home. The lilies lined the altar and the sanctuary stairwell. The Easter church service was packed with parishioners—some only seen on Easter or Christmas. Judy spotted a lily sitting on the bottom step.

It was healthy and two flowers were beginning to bloom. But a little girl, dressed in a long, pink, polka-dot dress and wearing white, patent-leather shoes, grabbed it. "Mom, this is for you," the little girl said as she handed the plant to her mother.

Judy was touched. She was happy the mother had such a loving daughter. She looked for another plant. But nothing was left except one wilted lily. It was on the top step.

She walked up the stairs and picked it up. "Water and fertilizer may turn it around," she thought. Judy put the lily in the car's passenger seat and drove home.

Judy attended the late service. Her husband, John, and sons, Patrick and Don, attended the sunrise service. John and Patrick were cleaning the bathroom when Judy arrived home. Don was unable to help because he was autistic.

Baked beans, waiting to be cooked, and a Jell-O salad were in the refrigerator. The smell of the turkey cooking filled the air. Her two older sons, four grandchildren and Judy's mother, Doris, and Aunt Barbara soon would arrive. Judy was glad her aunt was able to make it. A month earlier she was in the hospital with an asthma attack.

Judy put the lily on the kitchen table. Her oldest son Tom, his wife Jennifer, and their daughters Marie and Amber arrived. The family was good about helping Judy with the last minute details, such as setting the table, filling the glass pitcher with ice cubes and water and placing the salt and pepper shakers on the table.

Granddaughter Marie was the first to see the plant. "Grandma, it looks dead," she said.

"I think it will be fine once I give it plenty of water and fertilizer," Judy responded.

A short time later the rest of the family arrived, each noticing the wilted plant. The wilted lily became the focus of the Easter dinner conversation. "Maybe if you learn CPR you could breathe new life into it," her son Abe quipped.

She took the joking good-naturedly. After everyone left, she looked over at the plant and wondered if indeed she could save it. "The wilted leaves and brown stems did seem beyond recovery," she thought.

She went to the garage. There on a bottom shelf was some fertilizer. Judy worked it into the soil and added some rain water, collected in an outside bucket. Judy continued to care for the plant. She even talked to it as some experts recommended.

"You have a green thumb," her husband said, "but saving this plant is going to be impossible." Judy though, still hoped her tender-loving care could turn it around. It didn't.

Tears streamed down Judy's cheeks as she picked up the dead plant. She knew she should throw it away, but she couldn't. You see the wilted lily reminded her of her imperfect, handicapped son.

Many people wondered why the couple did not put Don in an institution. But Judy and John loved him. They vowed to take care of him until their health no longer allowed them to do so. *God also loves us, even though we too are imperfect.*

A Child

A little child graced

this place

with fingers and hands

so small,

A fall,

A scrape and

a warm embrace,

are

memories we always will recall.

A little hand,

A larger embrace,

And time marches on—

Until one day,

A child no longer wants

to play,

Grabbing a bag,

And securing its tag,

To travel to the unknown.

Little Fluffy

Little Fluffy looked around his dark room. But he could not see anything. It was so dark in there. Fluffy was scared.

The room smothered out any glimpse of light. "When am I going to see the sunshine and feel its warmth?" he asked. But, no one could hear Fluffy's timid, squeaky voice.

His mother and father seemed to have deserted him. "Where is my Mommy?" he asked. "Never have I seen her face or touched her. Where is my Daddy? He also never is around." Once, he thought, he heard a male voice. But it was just the wind.

"Why am I always alone? Where is the love that I know exists?" he cried into the darkness.

Fluffy was so weak he could not lift his head or walk. Yet, he felt heat permeating his cell. It kept him warm and helped him gather strength.

One day he lifted his head. Then he took a step. He was getting stronger. He, however, still wondered about his parents. "Why do they not want to see me?" he thought.

With each day, Fluffy continued to gather strength until one day he saw a ray of light. Fluffy crawled toward it and broke open his shell. Fluffy was a little rooster.

He had been developing inside that egg. His mother sat on that egg for a long time. Her motherly love kept him warm and helped him become strong. That's how he had enough strength to break through his shell. *Our Father's love also keeps us warm, helps us develop and gives us strength.*

The grass withereth,

the flower fadeth:

but the word

of our God

shall stand for ever.

(ISAIAH 40:8)

Rose's Flower Garden

Rose strolled down the garden path. The sun peaked through the charcoal-gray clouds. The thunderstorm left water droplets upon the grass. Rose touched the grass and rubbed her hands together. The water was cool; spring had arrived. But Rose's spirit did not match the spring that should have been in her step.

Rose was in a deep depression. It started with the antagonism that engulfed the workplace. Two co-workers constantly criticized her, and her boss condoned their behavior.

Then her husband Scott developed a kidney disease. There was no cure. He died Feb. 25th—the day the couple would have celebrated their 30th wedding anniversary. "If only I could see him once more," she thought.

Rose looked over at her flower bed. The irises, in rich colors of purple and white, lined the back of her garden. Flower gardening was her hobby, and she usually spent up to four hours a day weeding and watering the plants.

The lilac bush stood in the middle of the garden. Its fragrance filled the air. People often told her that seeing the flowers in bloom was one of their greatest pleasures. Rose planned to plant Joseph's Coat and Queen Elizabeth climbing rose bushes. Now, though, she did not know if she had the heart to do it. Rose looked forward to working the soil, taking solace in the work and what God produced.

Rose stepped on the concrete blocks surrounding her

garden. Scott worked hard to place each block a foot apart. The sun's rays sparkled upon the walkway.

Rose's jeans were covered with mud. She stooped down to brush it off. Then she looked up. There was a rainbow.

That rainbow reminded her of God's promise to restore the earth after the worldwide flood.[11] "God also will restore my life," she thought. She smiled. Then walked toward her house.

Notes

1. Nitsick, Janet. "Autistic sons bring struggles, joy." Originally was published in the Fremont Tribune 1 June 2002, sec. A1.

2. California State Firefighters' Association Steamer Team. publicsafety.net and The San Diego Paramedics. Summer 2005. <http://www.publicsafety.net/csfa_steamer.htm>.

3. Dice, Harry E. History of Omaha Fire Department 1860–1960. 1965.

4. Fire Dogs and Fire House. San Diego Paramedics. Summer 2005. <http://www.publicsafety.net/dalmatian.htm>.

5. The History/125th Ashland University. Summer 2005. <http://history.ashland.edu/history.asp?page=3.

6. Horse Information/Feeding and Watering Horse. Summer 2005.<http://www.frontrangefrenzy.com/horse-information/horse-feeding-and-watering.htm1.

7. Omaha Fire Department Collection from 1878–1994. Douglas County Historical Society.

8. 150!-Omaha's Birthday Celebration. Summer 2005. <http://www.omahabirthday.com/omaha-facts.asp>.

9. Elliott, Charlotte. Hymn, "Just As I Am," fifth verse.

10. Nitsick, Janet. "This day will always be special." Originally was published as a column in the Fremont Tribune 11 June, 2003, sec. A4.

11. The Bible. Genesis 9:7–17.

Bio

Author Janet Syas Nitsick is the daughter of former Nebraska State Senator George Syas, who served 26 years in the Unicameral and died Feb. 7, 1997. He was well-respected for his knowledge of Nebraska's constitution. Janet is a former language-arts teacher and worked as a journalist the last five years. Janet's passion for writing began as a child when she wrote to overcome her shyness. She earned her Bachelor of Arts degree from Omaha's College of St. Mary in 1995 after returning to school as a nontraditional student. She and husband, Paul Nitsick, a former postal employee, live in Springfield, Neb., with their two autistic sons. Readers can get a glimpse of the joys and struggles of raising these special-needs children through several personal stories included in *Seasons of the Soul.* Janet also has two grown sons and four grandchildren.

TATE PUBLISHING, LLC

Tate Publishing is committed to excellence in the publishing industry. Our staff of highly trained professionals—editors, graphic designers, and marketing personnel—work together to produce the very finest book products available. The company reflects in every aspect the philosophy established by the founders based on Psalms 68:11, "The Lord gave the word and great was the company of those who published it."

If you would like further information, please call
1.888.361.9473
or visit our website at
www.tatepublishing.com

Tate Publishing LLC
127 E. Trade Center Terrace
Mustang, Oklahoma 73064 USA